MERMAIDS EXPLAINED

Mermaids Explained

POEMS

Christopher Reid

EDITED AND SELECTED
WITH A FOREWORD BY
CHARLES SIMIC

HARCOURT, INC.
New York   San Diego   London

Poems in this edition were first published in various editions in England
by Faber and Faber Limited and Oxford University Press.

www.harcourt.com

Library of Congress Cataloging-in-Publication Data
Reid, Christopher.
Mermaids explained: poems, 1976–1996/Christopher Reid; edited and selected
with a foreword by Charles Simic.—1st ed.
p.   cm.
ISBN 0-15-100106-5
I. Simic, Charles, 1938– II. Title.
PR6068.E426 M4 2001
821'.914—dc21   00-053922

Text set in Bembo
Designed by Adam B. Bohannon

First U.S. edition
K J I H G F E D C B A

Printed in the United States of America

CONTENTS

Patchwork

Mermaids Explained

AUTHOR'S NOTE

My warmest thanks to Charles Simic for undertaking the selection of these poems: an act of true generosity, performed with a care and sensitivity that have touched me deeply.

Some of the volumes from which the poems are taken carried dedications when they were first published: *Pea Soup* to my wife, Lucinda; *Katerina Brac* to my late friends Het and Bertie Brookes; *In the Echoey Tunnel* to my parents. It is important to me to invoke their names again as this book goes out to a different readership.

FOREWORD

There's a lot of travel in Christopher Reid's poems, and there has been a lot of travel in his life. He was born in Hong Kong in 1949. His father was in the oil business, so when Reid was not in boarding school in England, he spent his holidays in places like Qatar, Aden, Sri Lanka, and Ethiopia. Reid was educated at Oxford and worked for many years as a freelance journalist in literature and art, and finally as a poetry editor in a publishing house. His first book of poems, *Arcadia,* came out in 1979 when he was thirty years old. Since then he has published four more. With Craig Raine, Reid was the cofounder of the so-called Martian School in the 1970s, a poetic movement notorious for verse that seemed to consist of nothing else but a string of startling images intended to shock the unsuspecting readers. Poetry is always in need of new eyes and ears, and the poetic image is the place where discoveries usually manifest themselves.

> Welcome to our peaceable kingdom,
> where baby lies down with the tiger rug
>
> and bumblebees roll over like puppies
> inside foxglove bells . . .

Reid's strongly visual early poems at times remind me of the iconography of primitive painters. In place of wild beasts and nudes disporting themselves in Rousseau's jungles, or placid cows and lions lounging in Edward Hicks' meadows, the poet shows off a new species of similes and metaphors. Strange comparisons give birth to surprising images; the unsuspected kinship between diverse things is revealed until the poem becomes, as it were, a heaven of the imagination.

> The butcher
> opens his glass door like St. Peter,
>
> as angels heave in flanks of pork
> that are strung with ribs like enormous harps.

Does that mean his poetry is a holiday from reality? Not at all. The truth is, we can only see clearly with the help of the imagination. The imagery in his poems may strike us as extravagant, but Reid is not after surface effects. "I like things to be accurate," he has written. He cares how things really look.

Reid's poems often sound like letters home and official reports from a visitor to a far-off exotic country. That foreign country, of course, is usually no farther than his living room or his London neighborhood. As he says in a poem appropriately called "The Ambassador":

> Life in this narrow neck
> of the galaxy reads like a rebus—
> one damned, inscrutable
> poser after another.
> The planet surface is cluttered
> with objects . . .

The extraordinariness of the ordinary is his subject. He writes mostly short poems where the placement of each word and a sense of timing are all-important. This poet's mission is not to save the world but the word. The humor in the poems—and Reid is a very funny poet—comes out of a kind of cosmic discrepancy between the lone individual trying to make sense of his existence and all the rest of it. As Russell Edson said, "The sense of the funny is the true sense of the tragic. That's what *funny* is all about." To make us think, Reid makes us laugh first.

In *Katerina Brac* (1985), his third book of poems, he invents a character by that name, a poet from an unnamed Eastern European country whose poems Reid has supposedly translated into English. The verbal lushness of his early poems is replaced by a style that has the feel of literal translations from an unknown original. "I write poems to make the best of what I have," Brac says. It's not very much. She has gone to live in a small village, presumably to escape the political pressures in the capital. Her poems speak of what in the march of history are usually regarded as "unimportant" events. This is poetry, one says to oneself, written in times of evil in a deeply unhappy country. Here is an individual, like countless others, who is paying for the folly, the fascination with power and murder, of some of her fellow countrymen. The air of looming menace gives the poems genuine eloquence and poignancy.

Reid is not an easy poet to characterize. He likes disguises, playing different roles, trying out various voices. While some poets seek the absolute, Reid delights in metamorphosis. He can also be unflinchingly direct. The long poem "Survival: A Patchwork," from *In the Echoey Tunnel* (1991), deals with the difficult period in which his wife battled breast cancer. The poem is an homage to her quilt-making, a plea to be taught the secret of patchwork, how to make fragments of their lives fit together. I can't think of a wiser or more moving meditation on love and marriage in contemporary poetry.

Mermaids Explained is Reid's first book published in the United States, and it contains poems from all of his previous collections. One delightful aspect of his poems is their accessibility. They are witty, irreverent, sly, and executed with great mastery in a variety of forms. They are invariably great fun. It's hard to imagine anyone, for example, reading his poem "Two Dogs on a Pub Roof" and not wanting to share it immediately with a friend. Reid is like a good-natured, generous host who brings out the choicest morsels and wines for each of his visitors. He is simply one of the very finest and most original poets writing in England today.

CHARLES SIMIC

APRIL 2001

Black Bananas

Arcadia

In this crayoned dream town,
the chimneys think smoke
and every house is lovingly
Battenburged with windows.

A studious invention:
these strange, ecstatic folk,
who tower above their dwellings
and whose trees are deckled biscuits,

nuggeted with fruit.
As they step among the traffic
that lurches down the road
on its long sum of noughts,

they look like damaged packages,
targets for pin limbs,
and yet they contrive to greet us
with smiles like black bananas.

A Whole School of Bourgeois Primitives

Our lawn in stripes, the cat's pajamas,
rain on a sultry afternoon

and the drenching, mnemonic smell this brings us
surging out of the heart of the garden:

these are the sacraments and luxuries
we could not do without.

Welcome to our peaceable kingdom,
where baby lies down with the tiger rug

and bumblebees roll over like puppies
inside foxglove bells . . .

Here is a sofa, hung by chains
from a gaudy awning.

Two puddles take the sun
in ribbon-patterned canvas chairs.

Our television buzzes like a fancy tie,
before the picture appears—

and jockeys in Art Deco caps and blouses
caress their anxious horses,

looking as smart as the jacks on playing cards
and as clever as circus monkeys.

Douanier Rousseau had no need to travel
to paint the jungles of his paradise.

One of his tigers, frightened by a thunderstorm,
waves a tail like a loose dressing-gown cord:

it does not seem to match the coat quite,
but is ringed and might prove dangerous.

A Holiday from Strict Reality

Here we are at the bay
of intoxicating discoveries,
where mathematicians
in bathing trunks and bikinis
sit behind the wheels
of frisky little speedboats
and try out new angles
to the given water.

Everything that we see
in this gilded paradise
is ours to make use of:
palm trees on the marine drive,
nature's swizzle sticks,
stir the afternoon air
to a sky-blue cocktail
of ozone and dead fish.

All day long
the punctilious white yachts
place their set squares
against our horizon,
as we lie around on mats
and soak up the heat,
cultivating a sun-peel
that grows like lichen.

A restless volleyball
skips between four figures
like a decimal point,
but the ornamental beach bum,
who lives under an old boat,
picks at his guitar
and contemplates the plangent
hollow of its navel.

In the hotel bar,
alcoholic maracas
and, on a high glass balcony,
a pompous royal family
of apéritif bottles . . .
Ernesto the barman
tots up a long bill,
castaneting with his tongue.

Our Commune

"A jungle is a machine for climbing,"
somebody said,
and then set up this aluminium plumbing

to prove it. Pipes intersect neatly
overhead,
where most of us lounge and dangle; or sprout directly

out of bare concrete, with angular U-
bends instead
of branches. Very Bauhaus! We make do

with just enough room to swing a monkey,
go to bed
on shelves and indulge in public hanky-panky

like the true Cynics. It could be ideal,
but is it? Dead
bored, a pink-tongued gorilla picks a meal

out of his armpit, reclining as if
at a Roman spread:
his right hand mimes the cigarette that would give
        him

perfect pleasure . . . Spider monkeys,
who nurse a dread
of stopping still, play tag on their trapeze

and ignore the puny macaque that hangs
like an old, underfed,
market chicken from one of the exercise rings.

We study bananas and meditation.
That foul shed
over there houses our guru, the wryly patient

mandrill, whose yellow satyr's beard,
fangs, bright-red
nose and fluted cheeks make him so revered.

Auburn, olive, ashy, white:
every thread
of his coat is remarkable. His hands are folded tight

across his apron, but offer him
a hunk of bread,
and he'll show you his eloquent brown-and-lilac
    bottom.

M. Vernon

The butcher, tired of his bloody work,
has made a metaphysical joke.

Five pigs' heads on a marble counter
leer lopsidedly out of the window

and scare away the passers-by.
The vision is far too heavenly.

With ears like wings, these pallid putti—
hideous symbols of eternal beauty—

relax on parsley and smirk about
their newly disembodied state.

A van draws up outside. The butcher
opens his glass door like St. Peter,

as angels heave in flanks of pork
that are strung with ribs like enormous harps.

Three Sacred Places in Japan

PRACTICAL ZEN

Hush. Timber-smells. The grain and sheen
of floorboards buffed by unshod feet.
A dim chamber with its paper screen
and brisk ink-daubs, where the abbot sat . . .

This small pavilion affords
a full view of two cosmic gardens:
here, gravel combed like a placid sea
and set with islands of rude stone;

there, undulant moss as terra firma.
I thought that I was quite alone,
until I saw the apparition—

a monk with meditative murmur
bowing his bristle-stippled head,
to cull weeds from their dusty bed.

A COMPLEX SENTENCE FROM THE ENVOY'S MEMOIRS

I met the obscure god
of their trumpery summerhouses
in a dank shed by the lake
with its mad square dance of midges,

where dragonflies, stunned and coupling,
hovered above dead pads

and torpid subaqueous fronds,
and I looked into his bronze,

bucket-smooth face to find
some sacrament of the mind
that transcended all clutter and swelter,

but nothing gave, and I left him,
smugly beatitudinous,
alone on his artichoke throne.

ITSUKUSHIMA

On guard against the harbor fish,
a dozen anglers line the quay.
Rowboats, a few feet out to sea,
moored empty, shrug their bafflement.

Big barrel drums, salt-seasoned wood
furnish apartments of the shrine
that's built on stout piles like a pier:
I see the point of worshiping here.

Below, the tiny tender crabs
tango in shallows, risking land,
then dashing to sockets of sludged sand.

Green seaweed wraiths, a beer can, drunk,
are tugged by the tide . . . You Nothings, bless
me in my next-to-nothingness!

Dark Ages

This is our heraldry of dirt:
a dog crappant on a lawn vert.
A supermarket-till cartouche
looping inanely through a bush
must have been threaded by some child.
No civic wall but is defiled
by spraygunned mottoes, jousting cocks—
the clichés of the heterodox.

Stepping warily through the park,
a constable like Joan of Arc
obeys the rasp of airborne voices.
Headscarfed old women, breaching buses
like siege troops, go to their crusades
of shopping in the far arcades.
A bollard and a station wagon
have met like St. George and his dragon.

Wind blows to make the rubbish rage,
impotent in its public cage,
or take tithes from the estate trees.
A page of news enfolds my knees,
supplicating. God bless the fierce,
string-belted mendicant who stares
where someone's frenzied tights and pants,
pegged to a maypole, dance and dance!

Bathos

Yes, I had come to the right place: the jumbo
cheeseplant languishing at a window told me,
and the lift's bisecting doors confirmed it.

Emboxment and apotheosis followed
at once. I approved the fragrance of a late
cigar, while numbers counted themselves discreetly.

Time to remember the whole of my wasted life:
evenings of apathy; vague, extravagant walks;
the cat bemused by my keyboard melancholias.

And now this feeling, as if I had been deftly
gathered into an upward oubliette,
to arrive—where?—at a meadow of sulfurous carpet.

There was a young girl at her desk with three
telephones. I spoke to her politely. Magic!
I heard: "Mr. Dixon will be with you shortly."

A huge vase full of plastic flowers stood
on a ledge, where an old man, passing, bent to savor
        them.
The unregenerate minutes turned and turned.

Of Mr. Dixon's office, I can recall
the photograph of his wife, some freckled apples
and an alarming stuffed owl under its bell jar.

But everything else has vanished. Stepping out
of the lift, beyond the ailing cheeseplant, I
looked back and wondered if something important
   were missing.

The Ambassador

Life in this narrow neck
of the galaxy reads like a rebus—
one damned, inscrutable
poser after another.
The planet surface is cluttered
with objects: wherever my feet fall,
something gives like a gibus
or jumps away with a squeak.

Impossible to tell,
as it were, between living and dead.
An innocent-looking box
will suddenly burst one side
with garish laughter. From hiding
behind a babel of bricks,
a three-inch ladybird
creeps out on stridulant wheels.

Most of the populace
turn out to be ciphers, dummies,
mere animalcules of stuffing
and stitching. I talk to them
politely, but they, it would seem,
are determined to say nothing
(although, if you press their tummies,
some do make a querulous noise).

And so I follow a nervous,
diplomatic course:
keeping my counsel; listening;
attending rigid tea parties
with mad-eyed plastic beauties
and blotto frogs; whispering
and peering in through the front door
of the tiny bourgeois palace . . .

If I lose my patience,
forgive me. Yesterday
I kicked a troop of saluting
soldiers down the stairs;
but at heart I still adhere
to the maxim, that through a studious
reading of chaos we may
arrive at the grammar of civilization.

The Traveler

First, I plotted my course
by all the wrong clocks of London,
the constellation of friends
whose secrets I alone could read,
hoping by venture to navigate
a route to the heart of the dream.

But you know how every dream
is apt to follow its own course.
I saw the great buses navigate
the capes and inlets of London
and tried in their commerce to read
some entente between my friends—

the archipelago of friends
that spattered, in my dream,
a map too dazzling to read.
I was always miles off course,
trusting to currents in London
that only a fool would navigate.

The eldritch gulls, who navigate
with their far-flung friends
the rowdy sea air above London,
complicated the dream.
They were not lost, of course
(with an open city to read),

but anyone else could read
in their attempts to navigate
the diplomatic course
of conduct proper to friends,
a wild fear of the dream–
cartography of London.

Undaunted, I traveled through London
and, learning how to read
the prosy flow of the old dream,
I found that I could navigate
between clocks, buses, gulls, friends,
some kind of a course.

Dear friends, I had hoped in due course
to bring back my dream map of London
for you to read and to navigate . . .

Folk Tale

And then there was a mad astronomer,
the shepherd of a solitary moon,
who chased his tiny, pockmarked planet
over the hills for half a morning.

The countryside was his enemy:
uncouth heather and highwayman copses
kept taking his jewel and hiding it.
His only friends were the eighteen pickpockets.

Once he ambled into a nostril
of sand, that sneezed and sneezed to expel him.
He left wounds on grassy pelts
and green tonsures. He often drew mud.

From time to time, coming upon
the moon, diffident, snug as a mushroom
on dank turf, he'd take his club
and smack it back into the sky.

It must have had occult properties,
to have led him so gullibly over the hills
in his houndstooth cap and tweed knickerbockers,
feinting vague arcs in the moist air.

Katerina

Pale-Blue Butterflies

Once again, magically
and without official notification,
it was the time of year
for the pale-blue butterflies to arrive.

They came in their millions—
an army composed entirely of stragglers
filling the sky,
the gust-driven trash of migration.

Working in the garden,
bent on our solicitous pillage
of the strawberry beds,
out of the corners of our eyes
we saw the first of them descend.

What were we to these multitudinous creatures?
A point of reference
on the transcontinental journey
from A to B?
Hardly even that.

For a week they came
lighting on our favored blooms,
as detachable as earrings,
but so common
that nobody, except the wobbliest of toddlers,
bothered to try to catch them.

Yet it was not exactly
a mutual indifference.
I'm sure that I was not alone
in feeling, as I do each year,
that this would be the perfect time
to mend the whole of one's life.

Later, when the butterflies had gone,
we loaded our van with the last of the strawberries
and drove to town
to be given the official market price.

There followed an unscheduled
season of summer thunders:
colossal rearrangements
somewhere at the back of the mind.

A Tune

Stammered on a mandolin,
an old sentimental tune
from an open doorway in summer:
of course, it's only a radio thinking aloud
and nobody paying much attention.
Who can afford to lose tears over music these days?

I have heard the same song
in numerous clever disguises—
embellished with hesitations and surprise chords
by my cousin, the promising fiddler;
crooned almost silently by women in kitchens
to lull children or coax the rising of the dough.

And then there was the dance band
that came twice a year to our village.
My father explained the workings of the bass tuba,
how the breath was obliged to travel patiently
through those shiny intestines, before it could issue
in a sound halfway between serious and rude.

Its thoughtful flatulence underscored
both the quick dances, and the slow ones
where the men took the women in their proprietorial
        embrace
and moved about the floor with an ostentatious
        dreaminess.

The band played an arrangement of the very tune
that someone's radio is remembering right now.

I dare say it means something to you as well.
Amazing, how a piece of nonsense like this can
    survive,
more obstinate than any national anthem.
Perhaps they will dig it out again for my funeral:
a six-piece band ought to be sufficient,
with wind, an accordion, drums and at least one
    ceremonious tuba.

Son of Memory

So the Muse of History is a man!
I ought to have known long ago.
The clues seem obvious now:
those big black ministerial clodhoppers
jutting from beneath the Attic drapery,
the rasp of that sisterly kiss.

It turns out that he has never been comfortable
in the uniform of the Daughters of Memory,
preferring, when it comes to business,
the manly clank of a suit of armor
or the no-nonsense Esperanto of khaki—
understood these days all over the world.

You may have had dealings with him yourself:
the functionary in the dark office
scanning your documents for a slip of the pen,
or the raincoated fellow who, if you catch his eye,
pretends to be utterly engrossed
in a window full of identical boxes.

Plainly, one can't be too careful.
It's hard to trust a living soul
when even mythology is suspect.
I'm beginning to have my doubts
about Terpsichore's clumping gait
and Erato's fondness for barrack-room meters.

When the Bullfrogs Are in Love

On those nights when the bullfrogs are in love
and their ratchety bass thrum keeps me from sleeping,
I have time to chart my position on the map of the sky.

Under night's aegis we rejoin the universe.
The moon, the stars, the mating frogs and I
are linked in a dizzy rapprochement across the
       light-years.

I like things to be accurate, and generally
you are included too, although you are probably fast
       asleep
in your room in the city from which the stars are
       invisible.

Long ago I would have been happily lying beside you,
for all the city's conspiratorial mutter
and the stairwell that waited beyond your apartment
       door

like the deepest, most superhumanly patient of ears.
In the end, of course, we were separated.
Now I am back in the country, out of harm's way,

I write poems and make the best of what I have.
Unable to ignore the frogs and their gutsy amours,
I let them spin with me among the constellations.

Epithalamium

An intimacy
like the brisk to-and-fro
of small coins,
your fingers thinking.

Something as homely
as a cat or a clock.
But what you leave unsaid
sustains you
like the net of the heavens.

Man and wife
with your life between you
like a chessboard:
a palimpsest
of innumerable possibilities.

Annals

Someone ought to write
the annals of the villages
on this bank of the river.
Conferences, statutes
and the economic forecasts
printed in the newspaper
are naturally important,
but there is much to learn, too,
from the sayings of old women
and the deaths of pigs.
I wish to propose
that a trustworthy historian
chosen by the Ministry of Culture
should spend some time among us.
He would meet my neighbor, the patriarch,
ninety years old,
who lies all day in bed
under a patchwork coverlet
which is really a symbolic map of Heaven,
but knows where every cucumber grows
and how much it will fetch
at the market in town.
His oldest son is a specialist
in the science of clouds
and never gets the weather wrong.
Of his seven children,
five of them female,
there is none without some deep knowledge:

of the different kinds of *eau de vie,*
of the magic language of cursing,
of money, flowers, childbed.
Beyond them lives the village mechanic,
a pious and reclusive man.
He attends all celebrations, however,
where music is required,
playing his violin faster and faster,
before wrapping it up again
in a square of black velvet
and returning home with it alone.
A boy in the village
is learning the Bible off by heart;
there are bets on when he will reach
the end of Deuteronomy.
The priest drinks too much,
but will give anyone who asks for it
his recipe against mosquito bites.
Last year two notable deaths occurred:
one woman was lifted by the wind
and deposited in the river,
where malevolent spirits dragged her to the bottom;
another choked, it is said,
on a fragment of fingernail.
Our landscape is enriched
by rumor and the discussion of prodigies.
Every day, history takes place,
even when nothing happens.
I believe these things should be written down
and published in the metropolis

as a matter of national pride.
An eminent scholar must be assigned the task:
not someone who scribbles little poems,
but a lucid stylist,
a practitioner of unambiguous prose.

The Oriental Gallery

Shadrach, Meshach and Abednego—
three pots from the same kiln.
Their Chinese maker must have been pleased
to see them emerge unscathed from the firing.

He was in the position of God.
They were his faithful servants, showing
by their unblemished complexions and perfect poise
how Nebuchadnezzar can be outsmarted.

Forgive me if I prefer the pieces
on other shelves: bottles with cricked
necks, and the jar that dribbles
its glaze like a sloppily fed baby.

Even more moving are the broken patterns
of pots that wanted to be earth again.

History and Parody

Here we are, for instance, the two of us
on one of those endless walks we used to indulge in,
talking, arguing, sorting out our problems.
The itinerary is pretty much as it was—
the street outside your apartment, the park
with its statues of ridiculous athletes and nudists,
the Old Town and the stretch along the riverbank—
though some things may be confusingly transposed.
An impossible silvery gray light prevails,
but that is all right, as is the sense
of gravity's being skittishly different,
a bit like the mood of one of Goya's engravings.
What do we talk about? Life, love and so on.
You turn to me, using your old gestures,
and I am happy to listen, even while I know
that words are futile and that we are about to be
      separated.
In the park, the trees surround us like giant fans.
The paths meet at a fountain which has stopped
      burbling.
It is like being on stage, where the third dimension
is in short supply, but at least we are safe from
      interlopers.
How ironical now to be wasting our breath on the
      future!
I smile wryly, but when you ask me what I am
      smiling at,

I find I do not have the power to explain
a feeling so selfish and anachronistic.
There are the statues with their muscles and dimples.
They look so real, how can I persuade you
that none of this is happening or needs to be believed?

An Angel

An angel flew by
and the electricity dimmed.
It was like a soft jolt
to the whole of being.
I raised my eyes from the poems
that lay on the kitchen table,
the work of a friend, now dead.

It should not have mattered.
As the light glowed again,
I ought to have continued reading,
but that single pause
terrified me.
We say of the old
that they tremble on the brink.
I found that I was trembling.

Perhaps the black country nights
encourage superstition.
I remembered the angels
that had visited people I knew,
not hurrying past them
and merely stirring the air,
but descending with the all-inclusive
wingspan of annunciation
to obliterate them totally—
and I rose to my feet.

That one brief indecision
of the electric light
in a night of solitude
showed me how weak I was.
The poems on the table
lay where I had left them,
not knowing they had been abandoned.

Realism

I have an idea for a film.
It will begin with a birth;
not the conventional euphemisms,
but pictures of the real thing—
mucky and time-consuming
like some operation in *charcuterie*,
where the child is produced
with a great deal of awkward business
in its ugliest guise:
a little howling blood sausage.

At the end of the film
there will be a death
and this, too, will be shown
in every possible detail:
nothing omitted
from the final grotesque drama
of spasms and incontinence—
just the events as they occur.

And what, you may ask,
will happen in between?
I haven't decided yet,
but at least I can promise
years and years of realism—
what our people have always required,
but never yet been given.

Eyebrows Almost Spoke

Eyebrows almost spoke
and I smiled uneasily.

A tongue tip peered from its mouth
and I wondered why.

A chin shrugged
and I knew that something was going to happen.

An Adam's apple nodded
and I meant to remonstrate.

Shoulders were deep in thought
and I feared the worst.

A back dismissed me
and I went.

The South

The insects formed an a cappella choir
and praised God for his almighty heat.
Their song hung like a backcloth,
a seamless silvery tremulous weaving of sound.
We staggered about like new angels, amazed
at the dazzle and torpor of Paradise.

Lizards paddled on the walls of the house.
Some of the birds could speak a word or two
in our language. A black caterpillar
on its curtain fringe of little red legs
crossed my path by means of a repeated self-
        strumming—
a charmed creature, not to be crushed underfoot.

Fed by a system of hidden streams,
there was a rock pool, emerald green
by daylight, malachite at dusk.
We dipped into this chill element
as if it were possible to taste a little
of whatever spiritual existence we cared to try.

I hesitate to say that I was too lucky,
but what is one to make of experiences
that felt like memory even as they happened?
There were mosquitoes, but their gloating hover
never touched me, and night lightning
fluttered harmlessly at the horizon.

What the Uneducated Old Woman Told Me

That she was glad to sit down.

That her legs hurt in spite of the medicine.

That times were bad.

That her husband had died nearly thirty years before.

That the war had changed things.

That the new priest looked like a schoolboy and you
could barely hear him in church.

That pigs were better company, generally speaking,
than goats.

That no one could fool her.

That both her sons had married stupid women.

That her son-in-law drove a truck.

That he had once delivered something to the
President's palace.

That his flat was on the seventh floor and that it made
her dizzy to think of it.

That he brought her presents from the black market.

That an alarm clock was of no use to her.

That she could no longer walk to town and back.

That all her friends were dead.

That I should be careful about mushrooms.

That ghosts never came to a house where a sprig of
rosemary had been hung.

That the cinema was a ridiculous invention.

That the modern dances were no good.

That her husband had had a beautiful singing voice,
until drink ruined it.

That the war had changed things.

That she had seen on a map where the war had been
	fought.
That Hitler was definitely in Hell right now.
That children were cheekier than ever.
That it was going to be a cold winter, you could tell
	from the height of the birds' nests.
That even salt was expensive these days.
That she had had a long life and was not afraid of
	dying.
That times were very bad.

Apollinaire

As gratuitous as flowers
in the iconography of children,
bombs exploded
on the blank sheet of his mind.

When you gave me his poems,
the strangely fragrant French edition,
I was terrified
by such *boutades* of innocence.

An animating principle
that was not the same as morality
declared itself as I read those pages
full of love and war.

As if the God of the old superstitions
had taken a holiday
under an assumed name,
wearing a jaunty bow-tie.

Picasso drew him
in the form of a coffeepot,
but that was just one of his many
ingenious metamorphoses.

His exotic name suggests
that he was related to Apollo—

or Apollo himself, condemned
to drudge for a while in France.

Surely that would account
for the supererogatory Golden Age
of artistic abundance
when the whole of Paris turned Cubist.

Under his divine inspiration
poems became pictures
of hearts, stars, guns—
everything that they should not be.

I still have your book:
it stays mainly on its shelf,
but I pick it up from time to time
when I want to give myself a fright.

A Box

Imagine a box, not a very big one,
but containing the following indispensable items:
a bed, a soup bowl, a landscape of mists and birches,
the words spoken by a pensive mother,
the absence of a father, several books including
a dictionary with a torn spine
and the works of the troubadours, a small photograph
in which the wince of a girl in sunlight is the main
      point,
a document with a stamp and a signature,
a message received from the friend of a friend,
a journey by train, an odd-looking parcel,
some jokes, anxiety and a final revelation.
Imagine this box, which should not be too large,
then take it and hide it with as little fuss as you can
somewhere you know its contents will be safe.

The Sea

The tongue tells riddles:
it is as slippery as a fish.
The mind muddles things:
it is as deep as the sea.

We did not go often to the sea. Our few journeys
to the coastal towns were an awkward business.
Where the sea itself was concerned, we were divided.
I was stirred by it to a vague romantic ecstasy, while
        you
found it an ideal pretext for your bitter Lichtenbergian
        jokes.
So when I admired the gusto of the fishing smacks,
the gulls' volplaning and the little waves that came
tilting over themselves like ostrich feathers,
you expressed your horror at what you called
"that vast untidiness—like being told someone else's
        dreams,
or shown a rough draft of the world's most boring
        epic."
Our walks on the beach were always perfunctory,
        ending
with drinks in a café and talk about town.
I think of those outings now, and one occasion in
        particular,
when I went looking for shells that you described
as "schoolgirls' knick-knacks . . . maritime
        bondieuserie."

Later I caught you stooping too, and you explained
that you were trying to find "the most imperfect
     pebble—
a very different matter." I laughed and seized your
     hand.
There were many questions over which we were at
     odds,
but none so large or complex or important as the sea.

Traditional Stories

Shall I tell you the story about the ladybird
who wanted some new spots?
The old ones were working perfectly well,
but the ladybird decided they looked dowdy
and so she went to see the woman who makes
the pupils for children's eyes—

No? Not that one?

Then would you like to hear the story about the horse
who stands on top of the highest mountain?
On cold mornings the horse breathes heavily
and out of his nostrils come all the clouds
that fill the sky. But the ninety-nine jackdaws
who steal gold rings for the sun—

No? Not that one either?

Then shall I try to remember the story about the snail
who set out on a journey to the center of his shell?
You know that snails move very slowly,
and this one had been traveling for a whole year
when he met a Gypsy with a magic cooking pot.
The Gypsy said—

No? Are you quite sure? That's a shame.

Because the only other story I have is the one about
     the country girl
who went to live in the big city,
and you've heard that so many times before.

The People among Whom I Live

I admire the people among whom I live,
even though they shoot and bring to the table
the courageous little bird whose cry I have learned to
      interpret
as "Leave me alone"—repeated again and again
and each syllable released separately
like bubble capsules from the mouth of a fish.

Even more callous is the way they treat their pigs,
feeding them, pampering them as if they were
      members of the family
to whom they have given the rather grandiose names
of opera singers and *ancien régime* war heroes,
until one morning you see them prodding their
      rumps
into the bleak interiors of army-style vans.

But there is nothing false about such behavior.
This is the way they have always conducted their
      lives,
ever since their ancestors in the muggy glens
first trapped a wild cat by the elaborate ruse
of a delicious buck in a deep hole,
or bribed a falcon to fetch them a hare.

In every other respect, they are straightforward
      people
and have treated me with nothing but kindness.

Surely their sins are venial?
They do not skulk in passages waiting for the cage
that carries its victim to a third-floor rendezvous,
nor do they drool over a human heart.

Screens

Memory supplies
the illusion that one has lived.
The past is as flat as the rectangle
on which the specters of film actors,
transmitted there on the backs of dust motes
across darkened halls,
play their colossal dramas
again and again.

Do you sometimes find it hard
to believe what you are shown:
hero and heroine
wafted through a reverie
of harvests, committee meetings, battlefields,
to arrive at last in each other's arms
while the Orchestra of Destiny
romps triumphantly about them?

I do. And yet once a month
a few of us climb into the schoolmaster's car
and drive to town
to sample the latest offering.
It can be a relief to sit there
and let other people's mind pictures
cancel my own
with their peremptory flatness.

For the private efforts of memory
are even more bewildering.
How can one justify the mad system
whereby one is oneself the producer
and main protagonist of a work,
the screen on which it falls in ghostly light,
its only audience
and the very dark by which it is surrounded?

Sitting here now, I can identify
a man and a woman
in a small room,
and they are talking intimately.
At the same time I am perfectly aware
that the vision must fade
and my lack of a past be reaffirmed
by a great balking blankness.

Heaven and Earth

Drizzle-winged, rainbow-flaunting
harbinger of fertility,
the crop-spraying monoplane
swoops on the wheatfields.

It turns and returns
with a diligence and grace
that would inflame the soul
of any earthbound poet.

Heavenly visitations!
I remember how in the city
the entire side of an office block
would glow gold at sunset.

And I would respond like Semele
ravished by her lover,
or the Virgin intruded upon
in her narrow room.

Meditational Exercise

I stood at my window,
thinking about you.
Outdoors, there was the usual business
of a summer's day:
broad sun, the parade
of cumuli in Heaven
and perfect peace—
when, suddenly materializing
miles away,
a helicopter caught my attention.
A moment later
I could see the pilot,
a mere speck of animation
in his snooping glass bubble.

What, I wondered,
did he hope to find
in this part of the country?
My next-door neighbor
stumbling about his flowerbeds
alone as ever—
was he the object of interest?
An old, slow-moving
man of the foothills,
no doubt he would be there
until long after dusk,
wading up to his thighs
in the violet smoulder of cultivated blooms.

This was how he would spend
every day of the season,
preoccupied
with his great labor of love,
tending tight-globed
peony buds,
marigold medallions,
lockets of bleeding heart.
And I would be his sole observer,
caught up in my own
greedy rapture,
the illicit passion of the voyeur.

I did not want the helicopter
to see him too;
I willed it to stay away.
For a few nasty
vertiginous moments
it appeared to be dipping
in our direction,
but the scare passed.
I heard the threatening engine,
and then it swerved off again
almost coquettishly
back into the silence of the clouds.

And what clouds they were!
Incredible structures,
flat-bottomed, but above
as elaborate as palaces,

they moved with the gravity of swans,
each one a separate
world-skimming Laputa
enticing me
on journeys of fabulous speculation.
And if the first to come by
was not quite to my liking,
there were always a hundred others
following in its wake.

Then I noticed
that my neighbor had gone indoors,
leaving his fork
rooted by the tines
and topped off with a sweat-stained straw hat,
to guard his handiwork.
The helicopter
did not bother to return,
the clouds continued
at their stately pace
and I remained at my window,
thinking about you.

Lines from a Tragedy

Pale twin,
aren't you ashamed
of what we have come to?
Abject crawlers,
porters of heavy flesh,
the unpretty caryatids
of a decaying house . . .

Surely you remember
the great days of our infancy?
Bewhiskered sister,
we did not always wear
such slabs on our toes,
such smoked-looking calluses;
our veins did not always
bulge like this.

Years ago,
before the fall into walking,
we knew how to play
and to touch the world
with our nakedness.
We were as tentative, then,
and as sensitive
as hands.

Like a Mirror

To have possessed you
like a mirror
in which you glanced once,
pulled a face and passed on.

But wait: can mirrors
be said to have memories?
Yes, there is always behind the surface
an inordinate heaviness.

So these touches of tarnish
are an attempt to express
a little of what it remembers.
How sad!

I Disagreed

We visited the famous abbey,
its nettle-sprung ruins.
There was not much to see:
gappy crumble,
bare shelter
for the ghosts of clerics.

Here goose quills
had once illuminated
with their devout scratching
bibles as fat as suitcases.
How unhappy you looked!
"Dead, dead," you said.

I disagreed.
Looking at the neatly arranged
fragments of saints and angels—
here the peep of a foot,
there the tuck of a girdle—
I thought we might have been standing backstage
with all the props
and that anything was likely to happen.

Patchwork

In the Echoey Tunnel

The little girl squealing
in the echoey tunnel,

scampering and squealing
just for the thrill of it,

spanking the pathway
with her own stampede of footfalls

and squealing, squealing
to make the brickwork tingle—

how fiercely she exults
in her brand-new discovery,

the gift of the tunnel
and its echoey gloom!

And then what a cheat,
to be dragged back to daylight!

Amphibiology

Like old men frolicking in sacks
seals slither on the sea-thrashed rocks.

Why does their melancholy sport
exert such a strong pull on my heart?

I could stand here for hours on end
watching them fail to make dry land.

From time to time one gains brief purchase,
adopting the pose of a Grand Duchess.

In seconds, though, a fist of surf
rises to swipe the pretender off.

Repetitive slapstick, it has the charm
of earliest documentary film.

Stuffed statesmen and wind-up warriors
turn to salute us across the years . . .

Only, in this case, something far
more ancient seems to hang in the air.

It could be the question, whether to plump
for a great evolutionary jump

or stay put in the icy brine.
May the good Lord send them a hopeful sign!

Contretemps

One lunchtime two men got in a fight.
The first tried to land a punch, but he missed.
Next moment, a barstool tipped and crashed,
the whole pub dropped to a dead hush and a tight

little space like a night-club dance floor grew
around the two bruisers in their ungainly clinch.
It was not like the movies: there was no second punch
and no attempt at fancy throwing. All they could do

was to totter on the spot, mutually clamped, grunting
and sputtering oaths, until one tripped and down
they both fell, still grappling. Each wore a frown
as stubborn as the other's. It recalled something

I'd seen long ago in a wild-life program about
one of those grim, antiquatedly armored species
for whom the sexual act, through a whim of nature's,
has been made almost impossible to carry out.

Hotels

In the first hotel
I opened my wardrobe
to an ambush from childhood:
a sweet, tugging fragrance
I couldn't name.
Shuttered windows
gave on to a blind drop
and the portamenti
of amorous cats.

*

In the second hotel
I noted that the wallpaper,
although of a strictly
geometrical pattern,
was upside-down.
A hornet arrived
the following morning,
loose-jointed, like a gunslinger.
Then it flew away.

*

In the third hotel
none of the corridors
ran into each other
quite where expected.
My Gideon Bible
was marked at *Lamentations*

by an envelope addressed
to Mrs. Minnie Fireberg,
Utica, NY.

     ★

In the fourth hotel
I fell asleep
about nine o'clock.
Woke five hours later.
A woman in the street
was practicing her giggling.
A bottle smashed.
Dawn crawled slowly
with its traffic chorus.

     ★

In the fifth hotel
the complimentary stationery
carried the most
vainglorious letterhead
I have ever seen.
Why didn't I steal some?
The plumbing shuddered
in every limb
at the twist of a single tap.

     ★

In the sixth hotel
the phone was pink
and its weight felt wrong

as I lifted the receiver.
It was no one I knew.
Advice and prohibitions
in several languages
were posted by the lightswitch
in a passepartout frame.

Caretaking

FOR JANE AND BERNARD MCCABE

The seven-story trees
on the jogger-thronged hill
beyond your back garden
register the breeze
with a convulsive thrill
of all their bright foliage,
a lightening of their burden
that I in turn acknowledge,
seated at your desk,
with the opulent awakening
of my own nerve tree—
just in time to see
some strange woman beckoning,
her dog's doggy burlesque.

★

Following Maisie's
half-remembered map
of companionable smells,
obliged to stop
for the frequent delectation
of savory breezes,
at last we reach the hill's
celebrated elevation
and there for a while we stand
with the usual kites flying,

joggers jogging,
lovers snogging,
and London itself lying
in the palm of the land.

      ★

Book shut, light out—
then in the gap
before real sleep
you feel the hill
looming closer,
then closer still,
a dreamlike imposture
that brings the trees'
lulling furor
right up to your ear,
and the monologue
of a distant dog
who more or less agrees
with what you have always thought.

Consulting the Oracle

An old, slow and sometimes forgetful lift
takes you up to her flat on the eighth floor.
You carry in your hand some trivial gift,
ready to thrust at her inside the door.

It is accepted and then promptly hidden
in the kitchen, where you have never been.
You'd like to peep, just once, but this is forbidden
by the laws of a now fixed routine.

She comes out with the tea things on a tray
and you go with her down the unlit hall
to the front room with its museumlike display
of gilt-framed studio photographs on each wall.

Conversation gets off to a limp start.
The unreliable buses. Yesterday's snow.
What the new doctor says about her heart.
An aeroplane passes disconcertingly low.

You wonder why you've bothered, until by chance
your eye lights on a china hummingbird
and instantly she understands that glance
as an appeal. The oracle is stirred.

It was one of a pair. Its precious twin
was stolen by the soldiers. All the time

her uncle stood there clutching this one in
his big fist—so! She does a little mime.

With such authenticity, she too laughs.
You know that prim frown, that tilt of the head,
from numerous dressy family photographs,
most of whose subjects are, of course, long dead.

They can be traced from one frame to another:
the plump, horse-loving cousin who was raped . . .
the argumentative great-aunt . . . the lost brother . . .
the uncle in whose Daimler she escaped . . .

But that's enough. There will be more next time.
You bite a biscuit and sip from your cup.
Chitchat makes do until the wheezy chime
of five o'clock, whereupon you stand up.

And your departure follows a strict pattern,
with steps down the hall, coat on, and always three
kisses bringing you to the lift's black button,
which you jab more than once, jogging its memory.

Romanesque

The Lion of Adultery
comes pouncing down.

His eyes bulge menacingly;
his mane is a blaze

of little slick flame tufts.
Under his impending paw

a woman stands
whispering, animatedly,

words of love
into an office telephone.

     ★

You see a lawn
in Arcadia
or Suburbia.

Dapper, bearded,
two Centaurs lift
nimble forelegs to drum
the earth's taut tum.

With blithe smiles,
they represent

the innocence of the world
on a Bank Holiday Monday.

  ★

By the moon and padlock
it must be night
and a dangerous part of town.

One of the Unnamed Martyrs
hurries home
while, out of sight,

three club-clutching bugaboos
lie doggo.

They are King Yobbo
and his frenzied entourage.

  ★

A sort of Dandy Dinmont,
head cocked,
spouts like an orator.

This is the Miracle
(locally attested)
of the Dog that Spoke.

Out of the blue
he gave utterance
to all manner of mysteries.

The stars, medicine
and Holy Writ
were among the subjects he covered.

And what he said
his mistress jotted down
on the backs of old, torn envelopes.

     ★

The story here
remains obscure,
but the man and woman
who stand in the mouth
of the great, gaping fish—
horned and dragonish—
and peer over its teeth
as from a tiny back garden,
seem less afraid
than might have been expected.

     ★

Saint Quotidianus,
a taxi driver in life,
appears with his emblem—
a steering wheel.

He is flanked by the Angels
who showed him the true path:
one carries a trumpet,
the other a scrip.

Balloonland

In Balloonland
everyone
is given a balloon
the day they are born.

Freshly blown up
and with the knot tightly done,
a big balloon
is put into their hand.

A few words are spoken
by way of ceremony:
"This is your balloon,
the balloon of your destiny!
You are its guardian.
Do you understand?"

And it's no use arguing.
Red, blue or green,
yellow, purple or orange,
that's their balloon
and no one else's.
They are the owner.

So as time goes on
they watch their balloon
with increasing anxiety.
Can it be shrinking?

Is it less shiny?
What's that hissing sound?
Did they do something wrong?

Futile questions!
Some balloons
pop the day they are given,
others last eons
just getting more wizened.
If you're looking for a reason,
goes one of Balloonland's
wisest sayings,
then apply your own pin.

A Perversion

In the *Proceedings of the Royal Institute of Anthropophagy*
(last year's Spring number, page 132),
there is a most unusual instance recorded
of a man and woman who conspired to eat each
     other—
and would have done so, had not the laws of nature
     prevented it.
I heartily agree with the writer of the article
who denounces the whole affair as a "flagrant
     travesty,"
a "perversion of the established rites" and a "half-
     baked stunt."

Klangfarbe

At the first performance
of his twenty-minute sonata
for trombone and lightbulb,

based—so the program note told us—
on a reading of Jung's
Seelenprobleme der Gegenwart,

the most eloquent detail
and the one I shall remember
beyond all those whomps and rasps and splintered high
      notes

was the ping of the filament.

Dreams of Babylon

I hold the book
the one I have been looking for

it tells the truth
in a strange new way

syntax of pentecost
you barely need to read it

rushing to the bloodstream
of its own accord

    ★

Cubism's collapsing
house of cards

portending a labyrinth
yards and yards

no, miles more like it
of scavengery and botchwork

under a placid light
just so, just so

    ★

The irreversible machine starts up
and I am in the middle of it

blasting and pounding behind me
scraping in front

exhilarating
to be at its fulcrum

with fluttering fingertips
and tutting tongue

★

Seems we've reached
the inner sanctum

peacocks in a cloister
strut their stuff

they drag their gowns
with a dry luxurious rustle

gaudy poultry
of academe

★

A stocky toddler
and his sumo stomp

green ideograms
of a swiss cheese plant

in apparently fortuitous
juxtaposition

if I had a camera
which I do not

*

To mix a music
out of the night

an electronic psalm
that will assuage all loneliness

from the black hole
a choir of sirens

maximum babel
and the mumbo drums

Survival: A Patchwork

FOR LUCINDA

If I could borrow
from your intricate art
this one among your accomplishments
a patchwork pattern
words, remnants, savings
things seen and known

> not that old man's
> symbolic map of heaven
> a more questionable symmetry
> looser fabric
> pieced out and negotiated
> day by day by

with the occasional mistake, too
passages jarring
you know why
able to trace
even in lines not quite true
a yearning

> and from your patience
> if I could borrow that
> a more unstinting
> resource than mine

given to tizzes
the short hot futile sputter

patience that sits
at the end of the bed
needle plunging
tiny stitches
lips that mime or inaudibly mutter
the primitive arithmetic

needle and thread
plunging and tugged taut
again and again
plunging the glint
of purpose and tugged taut
steady achievement

if I could borrow
as you adjust
the gorgeous sprawl
of work about you
paper templates
jostled rustling

scraps of poems
on squares and lozenges
later to be shed
for a while lending

structure and heart
to your art and mine

★

To name just some
the African quilts
the Aztec, the Firecracker
the cream and white
and those two sumptuous trophies
gents' old silk ties

in art jargon
color fields
and you the unflagging laborer
measuring seasons
method and toil
terrain hard-won

as if to occupy
a Klee landscape
who once spoke
of taking a line for a walk
the pertinacious spider
knows the procedure

or you've seen a child
paper flat on floor
inhabiting
the middle of her own drawing

an elbow smudges
lines newly put down

pitched into the making
strange to observe
and an incentive
Klee again
that each should follow
where the pulse of his own heart leads

two pulses
inevitable variance
but music of a kind
the dissonant passages
mutually punitive
yield to sweeter

as when
on the allotment
your design
and most of the work yours
strip pattern
onions, spinach, beetroot, beans

we keep a distance
auspicious nonetheless
to look across
and catch a glimpse

through the beanpoles'
tackle and tangle

*

A fanning arc
of hose water plays
over the bean leaves
drumming rattles
the summer canopy
a gracious dispensation

you love this narrow
Utopian plot
I love it less
but love you loving it
nowhere level
askew on its slope

wrested from the clasp
of couch grass and bindweed
your discovery
a talent to nurture
blackcurrants and sweet peas
overflowing

who once disparaged
your parents' farm
ironic
growing to recognize

too late
its parched obdurate beauty

too late
the peacocks that shrieked
vindictive queens
from the garage roof
almond trees writhing
in the combustible orchard

hillside-tilted
under a milder sky
less overwhelming perspective
I watch you tend
with fork and wheelbarrow
our patch

when suddenly
a jangle flung
disembodied
over the rooftops
an ice-cream van
visits the neighboring estate

stop, start
its musical-chairs
arrangement of Popeye
amplified glockenspiel

conjures children
imagine them hurrying now

*

Best-loved stranger
when the mirror catches us
chancing to pass
embrace and hold
our most ridiculous
photographic grimaces

> looks exchanged
> is that it
> a picture of a marriage
> caught on the hop
> watch the birdie
> then burst out laughing

of course no simple
image will do
the frequently trumpeted
republic of two
with its improvised constitution
and merry folk culture

> or sometimes it seems
> obedient
> to peremptory swings

of climate and temperament
the jittery ménage
of a weatherhouse

sickening squalls
electricity shaken
by the passing storm
gulp of vertigo
over the unknown
the unknowable

your illness when
I took refuge
in writing poems
any other subject
you with your
great lonely courage

what then
two solitudes
the grave neighborly
orbiting of planets
signals dim
as the black hole beckons

no no no
won't do either
stop there
hush typewriter

listen to you busy
in a not distant room

Your new beautiful hairstyle
a bushy bob
like Colette's
as soon as I saw it
to meet the ravages
of unsubtle chemotherapy

       dashing, girlish
       and as it turned out
       luckier than some
       those poor bald children
       at the hospital
       their hopeless wigs

resented days
laid-up in bed
Floppy Mop Top
the harsh chemical savor lingering
in your mouth
on breath and kisses

       never again
       you say now
       go through that
       and I say

                    amen, amen
                    that you never have cause to

yet they looked after you kindly
the sewn gash
by your breast
less elegant
than your artistry
did the trick, though

                         and who now minds
                         the touch of asymmetry
                         Matisse's jaunty drawing
                         one breast hitched
                         its nipple wider
                         for a while

gratitude
for a life mended
yours, ours
rending of fabric
timely bodged
and, of course, anxiety

                         never again
                         you say now
                         though we seldom discuss it
                         I've seen you finger

the crude seam
painful feeling returns

★

Next holiday
fair stood the wind
down to Provence
our little red Renault
followed its nose
a spiritual homecoming

        slipstream blustering
        like a flag
        at my open window
        Normandy, Burgundy
        the Auvergne
        conceding in their turn

at which time of year
fields of sunflowers
the massed millions
somber umber faces
yellowing tatters
that gaunt stoop

        awaiting inevitable
        doom of harvest
        and in the vineyards
        grapes suspended

heavy as udders
on the maturing vines

pieced and patched
an amplitude of landscape
yielding to enquiry
guidebook and map
those dusty village churches
we love

where saints and Bible folk
cluster on the capitals
in their medieval drag
agog with life
death, too, shown
biding

jaws, fangs and maw
memorably registered
lost souls lined up
yowl their protest
spirits still recalcitrant
guilty of what

of merely being
like you like me
spinning through a countryside
stunned by sunlight

slipstream blustering
night miles ahead

★

Those unbidden moments
out of the ordinary
sentimental or visionary
who's to say
stepping into a field once
Mont Ventoux

   stopping
   there surrounded
   by the frisky parabolas
   of innumerable grasshoppers
   I thought
   no, felt

inexplicable elation
a blundering interloper
graciously made welcome
or just ignored
the crazy saint
addresses his insect congregation

   all part of the pattern
   spilt landscape
   hazy sky
   the car parked out of sight

and you in it
boulders, thyme

those moments
when the secret seems
about to be given
world on hold
what old Roberto Gerhard called
magic of uneventfulness

things just ticking over
take them as they come
whenever
as in Mbabane
nightfall
the fireflies puffing past

provisional and fleeting
annotations
of a great responsive something
from the orchestra
luminous generous music
or your art

luminous generous
the quilt you gave me
silk ties
jumble plunder

how many months in the making
that epiphany

*

Well, you've survived
touch wood
so far
illness, marriage
the lesser tribulations
we've survived

and this poem here
not much more
than to say I'm glad
an emulous tribute
matching and patching
the pattern borrowed

8 x 8
a dabbling in primal symmetries
hope even of catching
in the midst of it all
the drift
the changes

two bookworms in bed
slow piecemeal understanding
you once more engrossed
in your eternal Proust

the mark advances
a page or two

then sleep
or the arbitrary patterns of love
interface
of kiss and kiss
urgent fluent reciprocations
rapture answering

       and what of those hours apart
       overlapped perhaps
       by the insubstantial
       quick-unpicked-at
       self-deconstructing
       patchwork of dreams

your art
stuff of the day-to-day
single-minded creation
that moment near completion
when you spread it all out
on the sitting-room floor

       hardly room
       this tiny flat
       for the flaunting of sudden color
       almost to the skirting board
       you squatting in the middle
       smoothing it smoothing it true

Mermaids Explained

Fetish

I have in my possession
an angel's wingbone:
valueless, I gather,
without the certificate
of authentication
which can only be signed by a bishop.

I treasure it, however,
and almost religiously love
the sweet feel of its curve
between thumb and forefinger
deep in my jacket pocket,
the way I'm fondling it now.

Project

A fruitful line of research might be
good manners
in animals.

Start with the big cats:
the jaguar that coughs
before it pounces,
or the one that lays the bones
of its victims in a neat pile
after each meal.

Or again, there's the ounce's
night cry with its
distinct undertone of apology.

Epigone

The last sphinx in captivity
was a disappointing beast,
hardly worthy of the name—
with its unwholesome pelt
like a doubtful
jumble-sale bargain,
and wincing, bloodshot eyes.

All the same,
it was a genuine sphinx
and, once you'd tracked it
to its cage,
could still offer you,
if not some great
poetic riddle to solve,
then at least
a few fairly flabbergasting lies.

From Information Received

In the small crowd
gathered to watch
the mountebank's scandalous
last performance,
there were, I understand,
two people—
a man and a woman—
whose faith in him,
far from being shattered,
was roundly confirmed.

Detaching themselves
from the crowd's sullen
and self-righteous rhubarb
of disappointment,
they left that dusty
place and took
to the highways and byways,
there to proclaim
the "good news,"
as they insist on describing it.

For, in their opinion,
a miracle did happen:
the fellow did fly,
just as he had said he would,
rapturously rocketing
to some point in the sky

of incalculable altitude,
before seeming
to change his mind
and plunging back earthwards.

To illustrate
their abstruse message,
they have some bit
of business with a stone,
or any handy object,
which they toss in the air,
telling you to fix
your mind on the moment
when it stops and allows
itself to fall.

I don't believe
we need fear this cult,
one among so many
and lacking as it does
either clear moral precepts
or potent symbolism—
some ingenious gimmick
like, say, the cross.
But the usual precautions
might still be in order.

Stone and Bones

SECOND GENESIS
    "inde genus durum sumus"
    Ovid: *Metamorphoses,* Book I

Two survived the flood.
We are not of their blood,
springing instead from the bones
of the Great Mother—stones,
what-have-you, rocks, boulders—
hurled over their shoulders
by that pious pair
and becoming people, where
and as they hit the ground.
Since when, we have always found
something hard, ungracious,
obdurate in our natures,
a strain of the very earth
that gave us our abrupt birth;
but a pang, too, at the back
of the mind: a loss . . . a lack . . .

SKULL GARDEN
    Ewen Henderson's

For a brief while, you must stand
in this dour patch of land
and draw a deep breath.
Fragrance of life, death
and something more: the sense

of a dark intelligence
determined to conjure the whole
from a pitiless rigmarole
of making and unmaking.
To feel, within you, waking
the same idea that powers
the occasional, upstart flowers,
or drives that twisted tree
through its slow dance, is easy.
But what ancient seed was sown
to yield this crop of stone?
And why all these skulls blooming?
To know that would be something.

By the By

Through a helpful warder,
I soon met the legendary
Dr. Spillaine,
author of the *Contradictionary*—
that vast rebuttal
of all established
lexicographical lore.
There was hardly a word
whose accepted meaning
he had not contested,
and the whole enterprise rested
on his glorious disdain
for so-called alphabetical order.

Moment

For less than a second
on that particular day,
the human dead of the world
numbered precisely the same
as the human living.

Equilibrium . . .

And then a head came
into view, with new thatch
oiled and slickened
against the scalp,
eyes tight and a cry
packed in lungs
ready to tip the whole
dithering edifice
precipitately the other way.

Mermaids Explained

As he read the reports,
he saw at once
that all the mermaids
were dugongs or dolphins.

Their tresses were garlands
of sea vegetation,
or the billows they made
as they swam far off.

And what of the songs
that could lull and lure
impetuous mariners
to their downfall?

A tinnitus compounded
of wind and birds' cries
and something on the brain
too wicked to think about.

Nature

The gory morsels
television brings
and deposits at our feet,
as the cat her offerings
of punctured mouse,
disheveled-feathered bird,
leave us too often lost
for the right word.
And so we sit in silence
while across our screen,
through snowdrift and commentary,
gaunt wolverine
go loping in pursuit
of some ill-starred beast
to pluck from its scampering companions,
and the inevitable feast
with its ripping and ravening
is noted by
the ubiquitous camera's
unsparing eye
so matter-of-factly,
and with such a sense
of our being implicated in this,
that no pretense
of horror or detachment
will ever make do
for the lack of a spontaneous

phrase or two
by which to name and greet
the harsh event
and accommodate it between us—
as nature surely meant.

Dear Diary

Today my wife called me
    a "pompous old fart."
We were hugging at the time
    and did not spring apart,
though her words were deliberate
    and struck at my heart.

It's a fearsome business,
    this loving and being loved.
Would anyone try it
    if they hadn't been shoved
by a force beyond resistance,
    velvet-fisted and iron-gloved?

Scenes from Kafka's Marriage

I

A workman came to mend a cupboard door
that would not shut. My wife had got his name
out of the *Yellow Pages*. He did the job
in next to no time, and then, glancing around,
asked if there was anything else he could fix
while he was at it. To be agreeable,
we instantly drummed up a few bits and pieces:
a jittery window frame, some plastering
and a power point we hadn't cared to touch
for years. When I took out my wallet to pay him,
he still would not go; in fact, he's here now.
He wanders about the house, just tinkering,
drinks endless mugs of strong, sugary tea
and fills the bathroom with repellent smells.
At night we can't sleep for the noise he makes,
obsessive and rodentlike, with bradawl and
        screwdriver.

2

I have asked my wife not to argue with me
in public, but I don't think she understands.
This is what I most hate other couples doing:
flaring up at candlelit tables in restaurants,
or grimly bickering in supermarket aisles,
impervious to the flow of loaded trolleys.
To cope with the problem, I have devised a face

which can be switched on at a moment's notice
to cover any possible social shame.
I have practiced it for weeks in front of the mirror,
so that, if my wife threatens to embarrass me,
all I shall need to do is to brandish this look,
which is somehow both merry and wise, grave and
     debonair,
and the entire situation will be explained.

3

The theme of last night's dream was infidelity,
although it involved not much more than an episode
of badinage and hand-squeezing with a girl
I had never met before, but whose piquant, freckled
plainness made me feel especially tender.
When I woke up, I wanted the feeling to last
and so I told my wife just what had happened,
only putting her in this strange girl's place.
It was a bad mistake. She grew suspicious
and I at once started to ornament my narrative
with ever more spurious and irrelevant details,
either invented or borrowed from other dreams.
Of course, this served to make things far worse.
It seems unfair, not being able to turn
one's involuntary flights of fancy to domestic
     advantage.

Feathers

After the big fire
at the feather factory,
the whole city
fell under a thick
cloud of feathers.
The boisterous guffaw
of the conflagration
had boosted them skywards,
and there they hung—
a gentle, indecisive blizzard
for most of a week.
Just to step out of doors
was to hazard
feathers in your hair,
in your eyes, up your nostrils,
on the blade of your tongue.
Pollution or sacrament?
The cleverest minds of the day
applied themselves
and a hundred quibbling
tracts and sermons
were written and distributed.
The incorporeality
and feathers together
to some suggested
angels, exaltation,
a new order;
to others, anarchy, death . . .

Then it began to clear.
But even when that turmoil
had subsided,
the last of the feathers
trodden into a mush
like old snow,
for a while at least
some something in the air
continued to dangle and vex us.

Fly

A fat fly fuddles for an exit
at the window pane.
Bluntly, stubbornly, it inspects it,
like a brain
nonplussed by a seemingly simple sentence
in a book,
which the glaze of unduly protracted acquaintance
has turned to gobbledygook.

A few inches above where the fly fizzes
a gap of air
waits, but this has
not yet been vouchsafed to the fly.
Only retreat and a loop or swoop of despair
will give it the sky.

Cycle

As she proffered
that enormous gin and tonic,
the clink of ice cubes jostling
brought to mind
an amphitheater
scooped from a sun-lulled hillside,
where a small breeze carried
the scent of lemon trees
and distant jostle of goat bells,
bringing to mind
an enormous gin and tonic.

Insofar

Put on this earth to sleep,
but with no true calling for the deep

problems of utter forgetfulness
or the lurid and scary mess

of my dreams, I have deemed it wise,
insofar as I can, to specialize

in those moments on the brink
when the brain is too tired to think

but moves, still, to a chant, or thud,
that could be the song of my blood

or some rhythm borrowed from the prose
of a book dropped as eyes close

and I pass, alertly swooning,
into a sort of pebble-beach communing

with the great blur of the sea:
a modulation almost visionary,

like finding myself in a land
whose language I do not understand

but from which I could bring back
some wisdom, some purloined knack,

just so long as I keep
it safe from the snatches, the deep

inveiglements of sleep.

Intelligentsia

The whole world knows Gertrude,
from the prose style
to the hairstyle.
Even Hem's embittered
and disloyal portrait
in *A Moveable Feast* will
never diminish that versatile
genius.
                Leo, too, is celebrated
according to his deserts.

But what of Phyllis, their sister,
who loathed all the arts
and would "sooner die than look at a picture"?

Isn't it time we heard more
about her?

The Thing and the Book

I wrote a thing in a book
which some people did not like,
and so they decided to kill me.
Now I have gone into hiding,
though I cannot escape my fear.
Shall I ever be free again?

Let me say it again:
I wrote a thing in a book
and now I must live in fear.
What will it be like,
to spend my entire life hiding?
Would it have been kinder to kill me?

They certainly wanted to kill me,
to kill me again and again.
But now I am in hiding,
so instead they must kill my book—
not the same thing, but something like—
and make the most of my fear.

Possibly they hope the fear
will be enough to kill me.
That is what they would like,
before I can do it again:
write some other book
deserving of a good hiding.

You might suppose they were hiding
their own, bigger fear—
fear of the power of a book—
in all this effort to kill me.
It won't be much of a gain,
but think that, if you like.

I don't believe that's what it's like.
I hope we're not on a hiding
to nothing, but time and again
I return to my deepest fear
that, even if they fail to kill me
and do not destroy my book,

no book so feared or disliked
will ever again find a hiding place.
So they might as well kill us all.

Two Dogs on a Pub Roof

There are two dogs on a pub roof.
One's called Garth, the other Rolf.
Both are loud—but don't think they're all mouth.
I've been watching them and it's my belief
that they've been posted there, not quite on earth,
as emissaries of some higher truth
it's our job to get to the bottom of,
if only we can sort out the pith from the guff.
Garth's bark's no ordinary *woof, woof*:
it's a full-throttle affair, like whooping cough,
a racking hack that shakes him from scruff
to tail in hour-long binges of holding forth
on all manner of obsessive stuff,
from pigeons and planes to not getting enough
to eat and so being ready to bite your head off.
He's whipped up in a perpetual froth
of indignation on his own behalf.
Poof! Dwarf! Oaf! Filth!
These and suchlike are among his chief
forms of salutation—and he means you, guv!
His whole philosophy, his pennyworth,
is "All's enemy that's not self"
(with the provisional exception of his brother Rolf).
It's no joke and you don't feel inclined to laugh.
Rolf's even more frightening: his *arf! arf!*
seems designed to tear the sky in half,
every utterance an ultimate expletive,
every one a barbed shaft

aimed accurately at your midriff
and transfixing you with impotent wrath.
You and him. It bothers you both.
The thing's reciprocal, a north–south
axis that skewers the two of you like love.
You're David and Goliath, Peter and the Wolf,
Robin Hood and his Sheriff, Mutt and Jeff—
any ding-donging duo from history or myth
that's come to stand as a hieroglyph
for eternal foedom, nonstop strife,
the old Manichean fisticuffs
without which there'd be no story, no life,
and the whole cycle of birth, breath,
scoff, boff, graft, grief and death
would amount to so much waste of puff.
You're spiritual partners, hand in glove,
you and Rolfie, you and Garth,
you and the two of them up on that roof,
barking and hopping, acting tough,
flinging their taunts across the gulf
of the entire neighborhood: *You lot down beneath!*
You got a diabolical nerve!
Who gave you permission to breathe?
This is our gaff! This is our turf!
Don't even think of crossing our path,
if you happen to value what remains of your health!
One false move and we'll show you teeth . . .
And so on. Of course, that's only a rough
translation, but it will more or less serve,
being at least the gist of the riff

that bores you mad and drives you stiff
all day long. Night, too. Nights, they work shifts.
One sleeps, while the other faces the brave
task of keeping the moon at a safe
distance and making sure the stars behave.
Which is why there are two of them. If
you've begun to wonder. As you no doubt have.
Then sometimes they'll mount an all-night rave,
Garth dancing with Rolf, Rolf with Garth—
though there's nothing queer about these two
      psychopaths—
and you're the inevitable wallflower, on the shelf,
surplus to requirements. Only you can't stay aloof.
Like it or lump it, you're stuck in their groove.
The joint's jumping in every joist and lath
and nobody, but nobody, is going to leave.
You're as free an agent as the flame-fazed moth
that's in thrall, flamboyantly befuddled, and not
      fireproof.
You're party to the party, however loth.
You belong along. You're kin. You're kith.
You're living testimony to the preposition "with."
You're baby, bathwater and bath.
So don't dash out with your Kalishnikov
and hope to cut a definitive swathe
through the opposition. Don't throw that Molotov
cocktail. Put down that Swiss Army knife.
Stop spitting. Stop sputtering. Don't fluster. Don't faff.
And don't be so daft, naff, duff or uncouth
as to think you're calling anyone's bluff—

let alone that of the powers above—
by threatening to depart in a huff.
They are your world, where you live,
and this is what their telegraph
of yaps and yelps, their salvoes of snuff-
sneezes, their one-note arias, oath-
fests and dog-demagoguery, their throes of gruff
throat-flexing and guffaws without mirth
are meant to signify. And it's all for your behoof!
So thanks be to Garth, and thanks to Rolf—
those two soothsayers with their one sooth,
pontificating on that pub roof—
and thanks to the God who created them both
for your enlightenment and as proof of His ruth!

Cobweb

Whether truly modest or not,
he wrote:
"I may be doing no more
than adding my one strand
to the great cobweb of quibble and conjecture
that now serves mainly to obscure
a proper view of the subject."

Lately, others less abject
have removed the structure—
the web, that is—
and erected it in a new place,
to stand
as scaffolding or support
for any whimsical, jejune, inchoate or passing thought.